Your Clearest Skin
The Ethnic Woman's Practical Guide to Taming Acne

Tamara Thomas

Your Clearest Skin: The Ethnic Woman's Practical Guide to Taming Acne

Tamara Thomas
Hatshepsut Publishing, L.L.C.
3145 South Atlantic Avenue, Suite 1101
Daytona Beach Shores, FL 32118

All rights reserved. No part of this book may be reproduced or transmitted in any form or by any means, electronic, digital or mechanical, including photocopying recording or by any information storage or retrieval system, or otherwise be copied for public or private use without prior written permission from the author or publisher.

Copyright © 2017 Tamara Thomas
All rights reserved.
ISBN-13: 978-1-935979-10-4
ISBN-10: 1-935979-10-8

Hatshepsut Publishing, LLC

To my mother, Pearl Thompson, whose lifetime struggle with acne became my inspiration for taming my own acne and for eventually writing this book.
And to my father, Anthony Thompson, who taught me at an early age that one cannot have progress without change.

The intent of the author is only to offer information of a general nature to help you create a personal skincare regimen. The author and publisher shall not be liable in the event of incidental or consequential damages in connection with, or arising out of, the furnishing, performance, or use of the instructions and suggestions contained in this book.

CONTENTS

1	Holy Sh*t!	1
2	Time For Change	5
3	Be Honest With Yourself	7
4	Understand Acne To Tame It	10
5	Tweaking Your Diet	13
6	Your Hygiene Checklist	27
7	Get Fit For Your Face	46
8	Skincare Misconceptions	51
9	Tools For Your Skincare Routine	55
10	Afterword	64

Hatshepsut Publishing, LLC
3145 South Atlantic Avenue, Suite 1101
Daytona Beach Shores, FL 32118

1
HOLY SH*T!

Have you ever had one of those moments when you look in the mirror and been amazed by what you saw? It happened to me one day after wiping my face clean after an oil cleanse (more on that later) I decided to try. For the first time ever, my skin was soft, non-greasy and – amazingly - blemish-free. Years of research, experimenting, and persistence had finally paid off. I had clear skin! If I were the type to cry, I would have cried right then and there. Instead, my reaction was, "Holy sh*t! I have to tell somebody about this!" Then, I ran downstairs to my laptop and excitedly started writing this all down.

To understand my excitement, you have to understand my backstory.

I'm not sure what age I realized I had acne. I remember as a kid going to the Dermatologist with my mom, watching as the doctor poked needles into her face and then going home with my own bag of prescription medications, but that's all. They were lotions and roll-ons and they didn't do much but make my face dry and irritated on the top. Underneath the dry skin, I still had oil and pimples, so I stopped using them. I remember a moment when I was about 12 years old taking inventory of myself in the bathroom mirror. I was a straight A student, I had friends, was funny and had developed a good figure; I would just deal with my acne.

In high school, I didn't pay much attention to my complexion. I washed my face with ivory soap, and that was the extent of my beauty regimen. Looking back, my skin wasn't so bad in high school; I maintained a very basic diet and I got plenty of exercise daily between gym class and my after-school team sports. So, my breakouts were minimal and confined to my cheeks. Like I said, I was too busy to worry about acne.

It was when I started college that my complexion became unmanageable. Being left to my own devices to manage my time, getting less sleep and less exercise (although I didn't know it at the time) really exacerbated my skin condition. For the first time in my life, I was eating all kinds of fast food and prepared food that I didn't know were further damaging my face - and my health. On top of the "freshman 15" everyone gains, I had prominent lesions and whiteheads all over my face, including my jaw line and, for the first time, under my chin. They were painful to pop and bled sometimes if I persisted. (I also developed the foulest smelling gas during that time. *Yuck!*) It was around this time I developed the now lifelong habit of stress picking – I found myself picking at my lesions as I read, as I studied, anytime I was alone trying to figure something out.

For the first time in my life I was self-conscious about my complexion. I was always aware that my skin wasn't perfect, but it was not to the level of distraction that this new acne pattern created in my life. The vicious cycle of pimples that I picked at that led to dark spots was bad enough. Well-meaning students (with blemish-free skin, mind you) would ask me why my skin looked like it did (I had no clue) or if I washed my face (Of course I did! Daily!). They would suggest I avoid chocolate or drink more water or whatever they read or heard was popular to do for acne. And I worked at the campus eatery, so this was constant. I wanted to die of humiliation, but the practical girl I was understood they were just trying to help (and probably a little bit grossed out that someone who looked like me was handling their food). I made a vow after that ordeal that I would never offer unsolicited advice to a fellow acne sufferer.

I was trapped and my self-esteem was at an all-time low. I really had no clue what to do about my skin. Even if I did, as a full-time college student working for minimum wage, I neither had the time nor the money to execute a plan. Oxy and Clearasil offered some relief, but they also ruined my pillow cases, sheets or any clothing they came in contact with. As a college student on a tight budget, I couldn't afford to replace stuff that got bleached or stained. I tried to change my diet, but with my schedule, fast and easy was all I could commit to. I simply buried my face in my books and lived with it until senior year.

Once senior year rolled around, I panicked. There was no way I would go on interviews with my face looking like rocky road ice cream. Armed with credit cards, I sought professional help from a dermatologist who specialized in *beautiful, clear skin*. He put me on Accutane and between glycolic peels he administered and my experimenting with vegetarianism, I had skin that I was no longer ashamed of (and I shed the weight). For a couple of years, I even had a nice clear complexion. However, I didn't have the money to keep up with the treatments and I had to give up the vegetarian diet because I developed anemia. My skin began to break out again. Mercifully, it was nothing like what I had in college (by then I'd learned from my primary care doctor I had food intolerances, so my diet changed) but having had a taste of clear skin, I became somewhat self-conscious again. My nervous picking didn't help either.

Pills… topicals… over the counter creams, even birth control… nothing gave me lasting results. It seemed the only things that were effective cost lots of money. I even tried colonics with good results (although I would not make the dietary connection until years later) but that too was costly and time consuming.

Somewhere along the line I got married (then divorced) and realized I hated my job, so my complexion concerns took a back seat. I went for routine spa facials and I was exercising regularly again so, like in high school, breakouts were minimal. Eventually, I became resigned to the fact that I would probably never have flawless skin. My complexion didn't stop me from dating or accomplishing any of my goals. I just wanted skin that wasn't breaking out and covered with dark spots. I wanted to be able to go out without having to hide under heavy concealer. I also didn't want to spend the rest of my life (and a small fortune) going to dermatologists and aestheticians. I got tired of relying on someone else to help me take care of my face. I hated being at their mercy, hated being on their schedule and hated that my medicine cabinet began to fill up with pricey products that never quite did the trick. I knew I would need to do some work, but not to the point that it robbed me of my quality of life.

I needed to find a happy medium. Somewhere between no longer being embarrassed at my appearance and no longer emptying my bank accounts trying to chase a fantasy that would continue to elude me.

It was at this point that I began my lifelong journey (albeit in fits and starts) to taming my acne.

2
TIME FOR CHANGE

If you're reading this, you're an average Joanne like me, looking for answers to the question you've been asking for years: how do I get rid of this acne?! Or maybe you don't have acne *per se*, but you have dark marks that you have to hide under concealer, or congestion (run your finger lightly over your face or tilt your head to the side and examine the surface of your face in your mirror; if it's raised, you have congestion). Either way, it's stress-inducing - which only makes things worse - and embarrassing and you want to change that.

Like you, I struggled with what products to use, suffered through cosmetic procedures to be rid of nothing in the end but my money. Like you, I sat at home missing out on events waiting for my most recent break out to clear up enough to put make up on and have it make a difference. Having people I didn't know offer opinions on my face, my hygiene and my diet (although they're not *completely* wrong, as I'll explain in Chapter **8**) hurt the most.

We live in a world where your looks determine how you are perceived and treated. People with clear skin are considered healthier, more attractive and more desirable mates than their complexion challenged counterparts, all things being equal. It's just genetic hardwiring, like youthful features or broad shoulders being favored traits in a potential mate.

It's also much easier to exude confidence when you're not worrying about what others may be thinking of your face or shrinking away from you like you have cooties. Even the most confident among us battle self–consciousness. Look up any famous person who has acne and you will find that they have struggled with their self-image at some point in their life, if not to this day. (They just didn't let acne stop them.)

The day I walked out of my last Dermatologist appointment several years ago, I was determined to clear my skin up and I did it. It wasn't easy, because life often gets in the way sometimes and acne is an ongoing battle. But I've always been inquisitive at appointments and an avid reader, so I had at my disposal years of professional help and research under my belt. I'm no longer self-conscious about my naked face and I can go out on the town without wearing concealer (ok, maybe not on the town *per se*, but certainly out and about running errands or having lunch with friends). My complexion isn't flawless by any stretch of the imagination, but the breakouts and subsequent dark marks are a thing of the past. And I can share my experiences with you.

Arnold Bennett was famously said, "Any change, even a change for the better, is always accompanied by drawbacks and discomforts." You're reading this book because you want a change. You must be willing to make new lifestyle and diet decisions and educate (or re-educate) yourself in your understanding of how to care for your skin.

3
BE HONEST WITH YOURSELF

Before we get started, I want you to be completely honest with yourself...

If you know you're the kind of person who does want she wants to do (even if you know it's probably not in your best interest) and who doesn't take advice, even if it makes sense to you, this isn't the book for you.

If you're the type that finds it difficult to commit to changes in your routine or lifestyle for various reasons, this isn't the book for you. Real change requires dedication and commitment to something foreign until it isn't foreign anymore.

If you're the type that is too busy to take time out for yourself and you put everyone else's needs ahead of your own, this may not be the book for you. To do this, you'll need to shift your priorities more in your direction, maybe even make some sacrifices to have time to devote to a new routine.

If you believe your doctor has the final say when it comes to your health and that he or she knows what's best for you in all things, this book may not be right for you. The only person who truly knows what's best for you is *you* and you're going to need to trust yourself and your body to see results.

If you've resigned yourself that there's nothing you or anyone can do to help you with your complexion because you've tried everything and nothing has worked, this may or may not be the book for you. Faith is the belief in something despite evidence to the contrary.

Somewhere in you still has faith because you decided to get this book. A leap of faith is what you'll need to start this journey and maybe, just *maybe* turn a corner. But faith without action is a waste of your time. I'll leave it up to you.

Finally, and most importantly, if your goal is perfect, flawless skin this is most likely not the book for you. Perfect skin is not necessarily unattainable if you have enough drive, motivation, time and resources (coin and access to care). I encourage you to find a good cosmetic dermatologist in your city or state and put your skincare in their capable hands. Today's best practices have come a long way and there are more options available for ethnic skin than in previous years (certainly in my time). However, I would be remiss if I didn't at least point out that it is unrealistic and a standard that you should not hold yourself to as an acne sufferer. At some point, there should be some level of self-acceptance. I'm not suggesting that you accept modest results if that's not going to make you happy. I'm simply suggesting you temper your expectations so you are not continually frustrated. And eventually broke.

A more attainable goal should be to control breakouts, control oil overproduction and even your skin tone; not drive yourself nuts in pursuit of a complexion that may or may not be within your grasp. Large pores, skin congestion and/or uneven complexion are often an inevitable part of being a woman of color with acne. And please believe, there is no cure for acne; you can get it under control but it will always be part of your physiology, waiting for the perfect opportunity to wreak havoc on your complexion all over again.

This book is for those of you tired of the continuous assault on your face by pimples, red marks, blackheads, whiteheads and dark spots. It's for those of you who want to take control of your regimen without breaking the bank and for once be confident in your skin. If you're ready to take back your skin and have a complexion you can finally be comfortable with, this book is more than likely for you.

Let's get started…

4
UNDERSTAND ACNE TO TAME IT

I don't want to spend too much time on the biology of acne-prone skin; the internet is rife with information on the subject. However, to tackle a problem, you need to understand the problem, at least on a basic level. So, I'm going to go over the basics of how acne develops.

First, there are two types of acne (or Acne Vulgaris, the clinical term for it): acne from bacteria *Propionibacterium Acnes* (P. Acnes) and acne from a parasite call *Demodex* that lives in your pores. The idea that you may have microscopic parasites living in your pores is something dermatologists in the US and Europe don't talk about, but there's a possibility nonetheless that your acne may be rooted in parasitic infection. Doctors in China believe that 90% of acne has Demodex as the underlying cause. Parasites live in and on the human body and for most people they are completely harmless; for others, depending on their health, parasites can grow out of check and create illness. I'm only mentioning this fact because I don't want you to feel dirty or become alarmed to learn of this. My advice is to see a dermatologist if you can for a proper diagnosis; insist that she take a skin scraping from you to examine under a microscope.

Most people shed the top layers of their skin as a course of their everyday living; people with acne do not have that shedding ability because of the excess oil, so the dead skin sits, trapped on the surface. Combine that with hormonal fluctuations (usually testosterone, androgen or progesterone) triggering your sebaceous glands to produce extra sebum and you have little nests all over your face that bacteria (or parasites) call home. It's perfect for them because they have all the food and warmth they need to multiply and live comfortably. Eventually the parasite dies, leaving its corpse and waste in your pores (not to mention their eggs, which start the process all over again). When your immune system gets wind of this and sends white blood cells to the pores, you end up with white heads, or pustules, depending on your level of inflammation. If the pore becomes open and its contents dry up and harden under your skin, you get blackheads.

Demodex Mite: Microscopic View Shown Next To A Hair

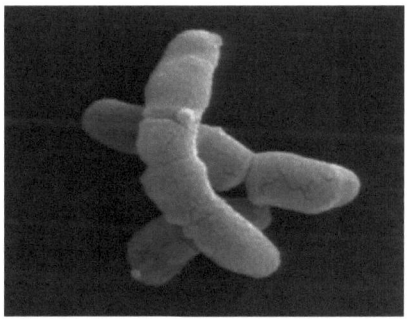
Propionibacterium Acnes: Microscopic View of More Than One

A few things are going on here that I want to bring your attention to: the first is that your hormones are sending stimulating messages to your glands. The second is that your body is producing more sebum than it needs to keep your skin moist. Third, it has nowhere to go because the dead skin that isn't shedding has trapped it, creating a breeding ground for opportunistic infection (i.e., acne).

So, what does this all mean to you? This means you should adopt a multi-platform strategy to turn this situation around and break the cycle. There are three major components to improving your complexion:

Diet
Exercise
Skin Care

They are in no particular order because all three are equally important to real change in your skin, like the legs on a stool. You can't achieve maximum results if you leave any one of them out because they all work together to help clear your skin. I suppose you can try two out of the three, but your results would be moderate at best. If moderate works for you, then pick your two components (preferably diet and skin care; many people feel they don't have time for exercise) and skip ahead to the relevant chapters; some improvement is better than none, but don't be crestfallen if you find you are not getting your desired results. For a dramatic difference, I recommend you commit to all three.

Acne is an inflammatory condition, much like allergies or arthritis. The inflammation is widely attributed to the foods you eat and their effect on your body systems, so it makes sense to examine your diet and make some adjustments. You're of course free to eat whatever you like but you should at least be aware of what foods may be doing you harm and what foods you may want to consider including in your diet. By the way, I use the word "diet" as a generic term for what you eat, not to prescribe some special food fad to follow. Remember, this will be a lifetime commitment; you *will* break out again if you revert to your old ways and it gets harder as you get older to reverse the damage. Whatever changes you adopt will be for life unless of course you decide not to go that route. In the coming chapters I will share with you common food ideas that can help make a difference with the inflammation that causes acne breakouts.

Your skin is a living, breathing excretion organ, much like your liver or your kidneys. It needs a fresh supply of oxygen regularly to keep it healthy, bring it nutrients and to help carry away some toxins. The only way that can happen is if blood carrying the oxygen comes to the surface of your skin. The best way to make that happen is with exercise, which gets the heart pumping and brings extra oxygen to the blood to circulate throughout the body. Skin that is deprived of oxygen cannot function optimally to defend against infection or heal itself after injuries. Your skin is a barrier and is only as strong as it was built. I won't spend too much time on this subject except to stress how important it is in helping improve your complexion. You decide what physical activities will work best for you; the point is to get moving.

* *

Acne prone skin has unique challenges and requires unique care. You must help it on the inside to improve its integrity. You must also help it on the outside to assist in healing and repair. And you have to give it rest and time to work better on its own eventually. I'm going to dedicate the most time to skin care because it's not quite as simple as *apply elixir X for 90 days for best results*. The idea here is to nurse your skin back to health with a supportive regimen and to keep helping your skin to help itself. It's my firm belief that the human body is amazingly resilient and that there isn't a thing in nature's bounty that can't help in facilitating human wellness; you just have to be aware of what's out there that can work for your needs. I will inform you of the many products and regimens that exist and share my personal experiences with the product if I've used it. This way, you can decide what type of products and regimen will resonate best with your lifestyle, your skin type and your goals. This is about a practical effective way to tame your acne; you should be completely comfortable with your choices or this won't be sustainable over a long period of time.

I should also add stress reduction (e.g. meditation, visualization exercises) and quality sleep as two other major components, but I know that may be unrealistic for many of you; just dealing with acne day to day can be stressful enough and may affect your rest. Still, I just wanted to put them out there in case you felt like challenging yourself and covering all your bases!

5
TWEAKING YOUR DIET

Most people bristle when presented with the idea that their diet may require change. I'd like to share with you what happened to me.

I used to get laser acne treatment at a spa in New York City. The technicians swore up and down by this procedure, showing me how it cleared their once problematic skin, so I bought a package of 6 treatments and got started, anxiously awaiting clearer skin. By treatment number 3 I saw absolutely no change in my skin, so I complained to the technician working on me. She went down her checklist of possible reasons for my lack of progress:

Her: "Are you changing your pillow case every couple of days?"
Me: "Of course I am."
Her: "Maybe you're not drinking enough water."
Me: "I drink plenty of water.[1]"
Her: "Then it must be something you're eating."

---

[1] In retrospect, I really wasn't drinking enough water. I thought 67.8 oz. of water (two tall bottles of SmartWater) was plenty, but I didn't realize at the time I actually needed more than that. See pages 23-24 for more on this.

In my mind, I ate a pretty decent diet. A pretty restrictive diet in fact, because of my food allergies and delicate stomach. I silently racked my brains and thought about the pizza that I'd started eating again even though I'm lactose sensitive. Since it didn't upset my stomach, I told myself it was okay to have a slice every once and again. I also have a sweet tooth that I indulge regularly because, well, you only live once, right[2]?

Me: "My diet is fine, I eat pretty healthy. I have pizza occasionally, but otherwise I eat pretty healthy."

I don't think this technician knew enough to tell me that I should not have been eating pizza. I never revealed my food allergies to her and there would be no reason for her to conclude that pizza was bad for me. She probably ate pizza herself. Hell, even my dermatologist came down on me when I suggested a connection between my diet and my acne (even though the Tazorac he had me on for almost a year gave me only modest results)! I think she was looking for a more obvious smoking gun like fast food or fried foods, neither of which I really ate.

My complaint was taken seriously by the spa manager, who was embarrassed by my lack of progress (yes, it looked that bad) and gave me complimentary services for my trouble. But I decided to stop eating pizza, just as an experiment, because that technician's comment stuck with me.

Weeks after I stopped eating pizza, the inflamed pimples subsided. I still had acne, just not the angry red and brown spots that dotted my cheeks and jaw line. (It would still be another year's time before I learned that my love of sweets was also a major acne contributor.)

---

[2] That sweet tooth would eventually lead me to develop Pre-Diabetes, which I still struggle with to this day. Take my strong advice: for your overall health, *please* try to avoid sugar. It's a serious addiction with disastrous long-term consequences to your system.

Now, the reason I shared this experience with you is to show you that I know how difficult it can be to face that you may not be doing something right with your diet, or that you should even change it at all. Food is the one refuge we have in a life filled with uncertainty; you don't know what cruel and interesting things your face will do from day to day or week to week, but you know that that lasagna in the fridge is going to taste delicious when you heat it up for dinner and wash it down with a refreshing beverage. Or that your family loves your meatloaf and mashed potatoes, so you make it every third Sunday of the month for dinner without fail. Even harder is when you have to cook for children; who really wants to make two separate meals? Or, worse, how do you answer your little ones asking you why you're not eating those fish sticks and fries with them? Our food habits are often what keeps us connected to our families and our cultures. It's called "comfort food" with good reason.

Still, I need you to consider the possibility that there may be things you need to add or subtract from your diet, which is why I call it tweaking, not changing. Your diet may be just fine, but it can always be improved, especially if you want to help your complexion.

Let's start by not working under the incorrect assumption that if you don't eat fast food, your diet is fine. I mean, avoiding fast food is certainly a major step in the right direction given the unsafe chemical processes that are used to make them today, but even a seemingly wholesome home cooked meal can mess with your complexion, believe it or not.

For example, were you aware that iodine, a necessary nutrient for the function of your thyroid (which manages most of your other hormones) has been found to aggravate acne when consuming more than 150 micrograms a day? Foods like sea kelp, seaweed and, of course, table salt contain iodine. It's not clear if sea vegetables will necessarily affect your skin (iodine deficiency can result in thyroid disorder) because they are naturally occurring. However, iodized table salt should be eliminated from the diet, especially because we consume so much salt daily without even trying. Sea salt, Himalayan salt or even plain table salt are suitable substitutes.

You might be aware of the relationship between eating processed foods and acne flare ups.[3] Or of the relationship between sugar and other high glycemic index foods and acne inflammation. But were you aware that consuming dairy products is also a factor?[4] You better believe it.

Most ethnic people are lactose intolerant, meaning they lack the enzyme lactase and cannot digest lactose, the main sugar in milk. Having milk causes symptoms like gas, cramping, diarrhea or constipation in those individuals, so they avoid it. However, there is more to the story for those of you who have no such gastric problems.

Milk is usually collected from pregnant cows and besides the naturally occurring estrogen coursing through their systems, there is also progesterone and dihydrotestosterone (DHT) an acne stimulator that works by activating the sebaceous glands. DHT is also responsible for male pattern baldness and prostate enlargement. Try to avoid cow milk and milk products like milk chocolate, butter, cheese and ice cream for example. Substitute rice milk, coconut milk or even goat milk and if you must have chocolate, eat dark chocolate that's at least 70% cacao.

---

[3] Source Article: http://www.doctoroz.com/videos/can-food-cause-acne

[4] Academy of Nutrition and Dietetics (2013, February 20). High glycemic index foods and dairy products linked to acne. *ScienceDaily*.

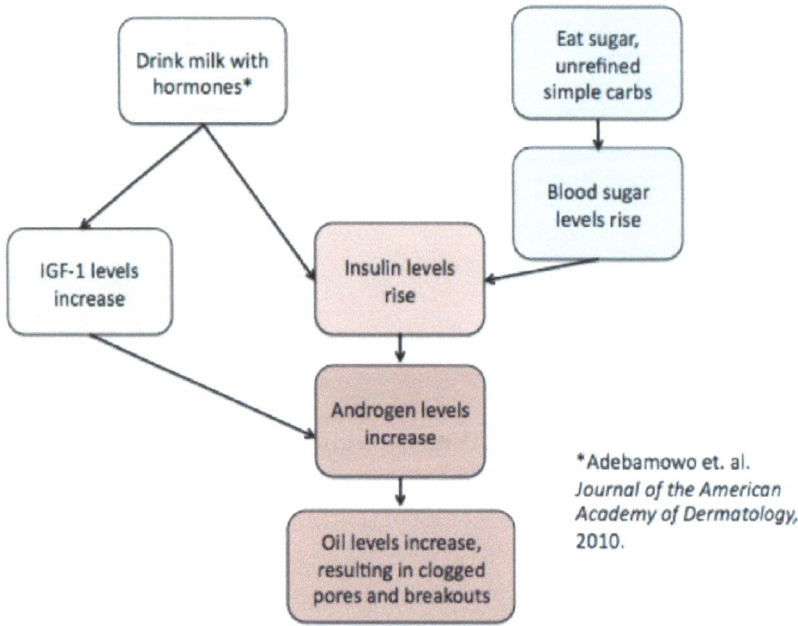

*Adebamowo et. al. Journal of the American Academy of Dermatology, 2010.

This chart shows you how certain food choices can negatively affect your complexion. (IGF-1: insulin-like growth factor, a protein similar to insulin)
IGF

The medical community is discovering that consuming gluten affects more people than first realized and that there is a direct correlation between gluten consumption and acne. Gluten, a wheat protein that occurs in pasta, cakes, cereals and other foods.

Sensitivity to gluten is a growing problem contributing to inflammation; symptoms can range from something as mild as bloating to more painful muscle and/or joint pain. In some cases, full blown Celiac Disease can result from exposure to gluten products over an extended period of time. Symptoms of Celiac disease include abdominal pain, constipation, diarrhea and headaches just to name a few. In acne prone individuals, active acne lesions can be a symptom of gluten sensitivity. Gluten that is not tolerated makes microscopic holes in the intestines (called leaky gut) that allow it (and other toxins) to flow out into the blood stream. The body recognizes it as a foreigner triggering immune response and it also releases the hormone insulin into the blood stream; both instances trigger acne breakouts.

Please try to limit your intake of breads, pastas, cakes and cereals wherever possible. Opt for whole grains like oats, quinoa, corn or amaranth for your grain needs. White rice is okay, but brown rice is better for you.

I would be remiss if I didn't take a moment to emphasize the importance of reducing sugar in your daily diet. Eliminating it is damn near impossible because it is in just about every tasty food on the planet. Even ketchup, my favorite condiment, has sugar! However, significantly reducing your sugar intake, particularly the fructose varieties, will not only reduce inflammation and help you lose weight, it will slow down premature aging.

Meat consumption has come under fire in recent years as being a culprit behind acne. I agree and I disagree. Any animal that has been tinkered with to create a "meatier" animal by using steroids and other food substitutes that are not part of their natural diet will result in a lower quality meat that is not healthy to eat. You can't cook away hormones or the prions of a cow infected with mad cow disease. The same goes for chickens fattened with steroids or fed antibiotics. Protein is a necessary part of the human diet; we need it for tissue repair and healthy skin and hair growth. We also need protein for brain function and for lean muscle growth. Meat that is fried, breaded or drenched with fatty sauces are obviously going to come under scrutiny because they are processed foods and are more work for our systems to digest and be rid of efficiently. Some meats take as long as 48 hours to leave your digestive tract! I believe that is what the meat experts are talking about; I doubt they are referring to lean grilled chicken, lean cuts of steak or grilled salmon. Also, I believe *how much* meat we eat may be an issue. Everyone's protein needs are different, but you might be surprised to learn you're eating more than you need. According to the United States Department of Agriculture (USDA) and the World Health Organization (WHO), the governing bodies that set our dietary guidelines, to determine your daily protein intake, multiply your *ideal* weight in kilograms by 0.8. If you are overweight, you'll first need to determine your ideal weight for your height. As a visual aid, a serving of meat the size of a deck of cards is a normal serving size.

I'm aware that organic meats are more expensive than regular meats, but if you think of it in terms of the money you will save on skin care treatments and products, it more than pays for itself. Alternately, you can get protein from non-meat sources like legumes and other dark colored and colorful vegetables. Iceberg lettuce has very little if any nutritional value, so try to get more nutritional bang-for-your-buck with spinach, radicchio, leaf lettuces, kale or collard greens for example. I like to put the last two into my protein powder shake and make what's called a green smoothie; I just thrown a big handful of leaves into the blender along with my fruits, coconut water and powder. That way, I add more veggies to my diet without having to cook them and decrease their nutritional value.

Allow me to point out some other less obvious diet challenges. Mixing carbohydrates and proteins can be bad for your digestion. How is this bad for your skin though? Let me explain.

It's true that we are omnivores, meaning we can eat a variety of foods for our survival; fruit and vegetables, grains and meat. The thing is however, that they were never all intended to be in the same meal together. Carbohydrates (bread, rice, pasta, cereals) require an alkaline digestive juice to break it down; in fact, it starts right in your mouth. Meat (and cheese) on the other hand, requires an acidic digestive juice for digestion. If you recall your high school chemistry, mixing an alkaline solution (base) with an acidic solution creates a neutral solution (like water, for example). This basically means that your ham sandwich with Swiss cheese is sloshing through your gut, undigested (think about that full or bloated feeling you have after you eat certain meals). I don't want to gross you out with too much detail, so let's just say the result is a toxic slurry your system now needs to find a way to get rid of. This means a new breakout for acne sufferers. And another. And another. And another. This is because each time you mix carbohydrates and protein together in a meal, you give your skin more toxic slurry to help the body try to get rid of. In fact, any food that you can't easily digest will sit in your gut and make a fine meal for the bacteria living there to produce toxic by-products that will eventually lead to breakouts on your skin (not to mention extra pounds on your frame). Remember, our skin is also responsible for excretion, not unlike our kidneys. Drinking more water can help mitigate this issue, but I'll get to that soon.

The good news though, is you can have vegetables with meat or vegetables with carbohydrates with no problem! You just need to keep 3 hours between eating starches and proteins to allow for proper digestion. A diet high in vegetables and fresh fruits (along with lots of water) will help you achieve better overall health including better digestion and a cleaner complexion (or at least fewer active breakouts).

Most people will go through their entire life never knowing this, because they have no outward inflammatory response. That is not to say it won't eventually catch up with them later in the form of other illnesses generally associated with aging. For the rest of the population, particularly those of us with sensitivities like allergies and those of us with acne in America, this is important to know now because the Western diet is very high in sandwiches, not salads.

Speaking of salads, many people have had success taming acne with a vegetarian diet. Eliminating meat from the diet and consuming only fruits, vegetables and grains has done wonders for the complexions of acne sufferers who are tired of the breakouts and desire a simpler way to achieve better internal and external health. Some have taken the additional step of consuming a raw food diet, where everything consumed is in its uncooked, natural state (ex, fresh fruits and vegetables and/or juices). However, you need to be careful to get enough protein from plant sources since animal sources of protein would no longer be an option. Combining certain non-animal foods can provide complete protein by what is called complementary proteins. For example, consuming grains (e.g., rice) or nuts/seeds with legumes (e.g., beans) can provide necessary dietary protein. You don't even need to eat them in the same meal to gain the benefits, just make them part of your regular diet. Research vegetarian and raw food diets to learn more and to see of these are options for you.

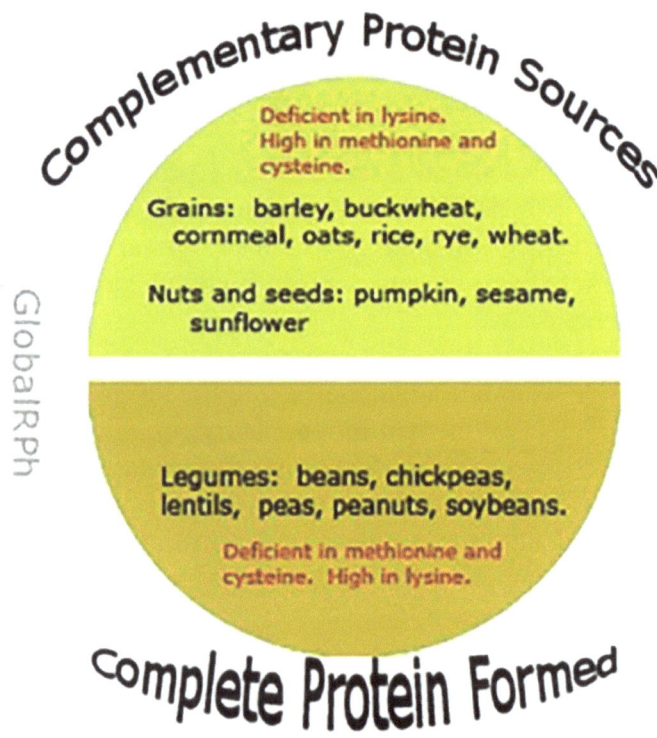

A quick glance at how complementary proteins are formed

    This all probably sounds like more trouble than it's worth. Keep in mind that no one is forcing you to do anything you don't want to do. Cheeseburgers, burritos and sausage pizza are quick, easy and taste really good! A submarine sandwich is a cost effective and filling lunch or dinner if you're a busy individual on a budget. Nothing takes the fun out of living like having to watch what you eat. And who says people have money or time for salads? They're not even all that filling! I get it; I've been there.

Let me put it to you this way: life is about choices. You can choose to keep doing what you're doing and continue to deal with acne breakouts. Or, you can choose to change your diet, by replacing one meal a day to start and begin to see decreased breakouts. Either way, the choice is yours and yours alone because only you know your circumstances, your lifestyle and your pockets. I've seen a hundred times across the internet women complaining bitterly about *Product X* not working for her skin and how crestfallen she is to not receive amazing results like others who tried it.

I want to reply to her each time, "But sweetheart, did you try changing your diet??"

Most breakouts are the result of inflammation. Inflammation can come from any of the pathways I listed in this chapter. It destroys not only your complexion but your internal systems. Diseases like Crohn's Disease or Rheumatoid Arthritis are examples of what can happen to the body when inflammation is left unchecked for too many years.

However, there are supplements available that can help tackle inflammation.

You've probably heard the term Omega-3s or Omega-6s thrown around in commercials and news articles. They're referring to Omega Fatty Acids (3,6 and 9), essential fats that are important to our diet but that our bodies can't make on their own so we need to get them from dietary sources. Of particular importance is Omega-3, because unless you eat a diet high in seafood, you'll need to supplement with fish oil to help decrease inflammation. Omega-3s also help keep the top outer layer of the skin strong and intact so that external toxins and pollutants are kept out. Omega 6 is plentiful if you eat red meat or prepared snack foods and is linked to increased inflammation when consumed in excess. If you use olive oil, avocado or nuts like almonds or hazelnuts regularly in your food preparation or as food sources, you're getting sufficient Omega 9's in your diet.

Another supplement I think you'll be interested to learn about is MethylSulfonylMethane (MSM). It's an organosulfur compound, meaning its sulfur is bioavailable in the body, and it's widely discussed for its benefit to hair, nails, joints and skin. MSM provides anti-inflammatory benefits and has also been shown to soften skin, making it healthier, younger looking and better able to function at protecting itself from unwelcome guests like opportunistic parasites or destructive bacteria. MSM can be taken as a supplement, but what I've read about this wonder compound is that the benefits seem to be more pronounced with external use. I recommend using it internally and externally (there is also the soap and the lotion) for optimal results, but if you can't afford the supplement, the bar soap and lotion are budget friendly. We'll come back to this again in the chapter on skin care.

The mineral Zinc has been praised for its role in helping relieve acne. It boosts the immune system, helps speed wound healing properties, increases cell turnover to reveal new skin and helps retain skin moisture, providing anti-aging benefits. Many people with acne are deficient in this trace mineral. Zinc is in foods like oysters, spinach and red meats. You can also take the supplement but look for Zinc Gluconate; it is supposed to be a safer formulation.

Drinking plenty of water daily is an often-underestimated step in taking care of skin. The human body is made up of about 50-60% water and is essential to just about every function in your body, including proper digestion and elimination. Water helps keep you hydrated, but it also helps to control your appetite. In fact, studies have shown that when people crave salty or sweet snacks it is usually because they are thirsty. Water also helps your kidneys to function better at excretion and keeps your skin looking good. According to the Mayo Clinic, the recommended daily amount of water for optimal health and organ function should be as follows:

Men - 13 8-Ounce Glasses (3 liters)
Women - 9 8-Ounce Glasses (2.2 liters)
　　　They also state that you can meet your water intake

requirements from sources other than water (like juices for example)[5] but I don't believe those recommendations take acne sufferers (or diabetics), who need to limit their sugar intake into consideration. Herbal teas are a more sensible source for water intake; add a half a teaspoon of honey if you *really* need some sweetness.

Most holistic health practitioners provide a more comprehensive guideline for daily water intake:
Divide your weight by 2, then change the pounds to ounces
(Ex: 150lbs ÷ 2 = 75lbs or 75oz of water daily)

I personally try to drink at least 100 oz. of water daily, including herbal tea; I've found this to be the sweet spot for me in terms of hydration and helping keep my skin blemish free. But not everyone should feel the need to drink that much. Whatever formula you settle on, I do recommend that you drink your water a half hour before or an hour after you eat for proper digestion.

Aestheticians and naturopaths take it one step further and suggest squeezing half a lemon into your room temperature, warm or hot water. Done first thing in the morning ½ hour before anything else goes into your mouth, this helps to refresh you, to clean your palate and to help clear your digestive tract from the previous day's toxins. Many people report having to visit the toilet after having this healthy mix (which is a good thing). Lemons have many superb health benefits aside from cleansing, but please limit the practice to once a day in the morning; the acids from the lemon can erode your tooth enamel.

* *

Making even small changes in the way you eat, including colorful fruits, leafy dark green vegetables and high-quality multivitamin supplements will yield promising improvements in the look and overall texture of your skin. You may also notice that you will start to feel better, have more energy and you may even

---

[5] Source: http://www.mayoclinic.com/health/water/NU00283

start to shed pounds as you change and tweak your diet to tame those breakouts.

Above all, please learn to trust your instincts; the infinite wisdom of your body and your skin will help guide you along your journey. You will start to learn what works for your skin and what your skin hates. And you will gain confidence in your ability to manage your unique complexion challenges.

Here's a quick and dirty list of foods to try to avoid, or at least eat less:

- Sugars (Ex: White/Cane Sugar, High Fructose Corn Syrup, Sucrose, Sorbitol, Malt Sugars). I found a great list of sugars at the Huffington Post website.
- Complex Carbohydrates (Ex: Breads, Semolina Pasta, Cakes, Cookies, Crusts, Muffins, Pastries)- They just turn into sugars in the body.
- Fried Foods – Hard for the body to digest, are artery-clogging and are inflammatory to the body.
- Excess meat – Hard on the digestive system, especially when processed, breaded or fried.
- Poor Food Combinations (Ex: Eating bread with meat or pasta with cheese) – The food remains undigested and ferments in your gut.
- Sweets – (Ex: Candy, Sweetened Milk Chocolate, Gum) – They are basically sugars and other processed ingredients. Too much over time can cause inflammation and lead to diabetes.

6
YOUR HYGIENE CHECKLIST

I know what you're thinking.

You're thinking I'm going to accuse you of not practicing proper hygiene. You're thinking I'm going to preach to you about how you should be washing your face. Well, that's not really what I'm here to do. I mean, I am going to touch on the best way to handle your face, but mostly I want to give you a checklist to go through to ensure you minimize your chances for unnecessary breakouts. Many of these you've heard before, some you might not have. Either way, it's better to be armed with information that can only help you in your journey to cut down on acne breakouts. As acne sufferers, we must hold ourselves to a much higher level of hygiene than others because our skin really reflects our health and wellness. Unlike others with clear skin, we can't hide our bad habits because they are literally written all over our faces.

Cleanse Your Face Religiously

This is pretty basic, I know. But how many of you have been so exhausted after a night of partying, or a long day, that all you want to do is crawl into your bed? Or you're staying over at a friend's (or boyfriend's) place and you're embarrassed to take your makeup off before bed? I know, I've been there – in both instances! With all those spots all over my face, there was *no way* I was going to let anyone see me without my Dermablend!

If you do nothing else before you pass out at night, it's imperative that you cleanse your face of all debris. Cleansing your face before bed allows your face a chance to attempt to heal itself while you sleep. Sleeping with makeup on clogs your pores and prevents your skin from breathing, which can lead to a new crop of pimples. Cleanse your face completely, including your ears, behind your ears and your neck, with a gentle cleanser. Your cleanser should not leave your face feeling "squeaky clean" or dried out, but you should make sure that all traces of makeup are cleansed from your face.

I don't want to tell you not to have a social life, but if the prospect of removing your makeup in front of others is too uncomfortable for you, you should consider going home. Your friends will understand if you prefer to sleep in your own bed or if you have to be up early the next morning; and if they don't, screw 'em. The same goes for your partner.

Please Quit Smoking

Speaking of a social life, those of you who smoke should really take heed to what I'm about to say here.

Smoking depletes your body of Vitamin C and E. These vitamins are essential for wound healing and for combating oxidation that occurs in the body (which leads to free radicals). When you smoke, the antioxidant properties of these vitamins can't do their job to protect your cells. Which means that pimple you squeezed mercilessly will take a longer time to heal and will not heal nicely. If you've squeezed ten pimples, well… you get the idea. *A hot mess.*

Smoking suppresses your immune system. Acne is an inflammatory condition for the most part, which means your immune system is reacting to the bacteria or other foreign invaders to your skin. Some studies show smoking's immune suppression to help some forms of inflammatory acne because it lowers the hyper immune response in the skin. However, I have not read these studies and it sounds extremely irresponsible to me to suggest that an act so toxic as smoking can have *any* benefits. Keeping your immune system in tact is essential to your overall health and infection fighting ability.

Smoking robs your skin of collagen. Collagen is the major protein in the body that is responsible for keeping your connective tissue together under your skin. When your Vitamin C is depleted, collagen production is interfered with, so your youthful looking skin eventually becomes thin and dry, making you look older. Any acne scarring you have will become more pronounced as your skin volume decreases and the connective layer underneath your skin loosens (think James Woods, the actor).

I don't want to be a Debbie Downer, but if you're serious about taming your acne, smoking is definitely a habit you should get rid of immediately. I know that it's extremely hard to quit, but there are resources to assist you in getting started[6]. Even being around a smoker and inhaling second-hand smoke can be just as disastrous for your health and beauty (which is why the Clean Indoor Air Act spread across the US so quickly and has even been adopted in some European cities). As time goes by without smoking or exposure to smoke, your complexion will thank you (as well as other parts of your body). You will feel better about yourself as your health returns to your skin, making acne easier to deal with.

I hope I've impressed upon you the importance of quitting smoking as part your overall beauty health plan inside and out.

---

[6] The Centers for Disease Control has information on help with quitting - http://www.cdc.gov/tobacco/campaign/tips/quit-smoking/ Check your local government resources for information on smoking cessation outside of the US.

Wash Your Hands Often

It's difficult to tell you not to touch your face. Shoot, it's difficult *not* to touch your face, so I won't even go there. However, I will advise you to wash your hands as often as possible.

Your hands and fingernails carry a load of germs that can potentially infect your face. On average, we touch our faces two to three thousand times a day; less if you're conscious of it, more if you're self-conscious. If you're a nervous picker (like me), you create more opportunity for spreading infection by picking existing pimples and by adding new germs to your skin's flora. Wash your hands as soon as you come home, before and after you eat, after shaking hands... every time your hands are in contact with something that is touched by others (doorknobs, chairs, or money for example) or touched by you often (e.g., steering wheel, keys, cell or home phone, appliances, toilet flusher handle). If all you have access to is hand sanitizer, then use that - and avoid touching your face until you can wash them. Use very warm to almost hot water and get a good lather all over your hands and in between your fingers. Sing the alphabets twice in your head (about 20 seconds) and then you can rinse. If you wear long nails, try to get soap on the under sides of the nails as well. Rinse well and dry with a paper towel; hand towels are not always hygienic because of how frequently they're used.

Clean Your Gadgets Often

We live in a tech age that brings new opportunities to spread infection that was once only seen in overcrowded big cities. We tap on computer keys and phones at work. We chat on our cell phones to pass the time. We bring these things in contact with our face daily and don't give it a second thought.

Use a cotton ball dipped in either hydrogen peroxide or rubbing alcohol to clean your cell phone all over, especially the screen and the keyboard. Use cleaning wipes to wipe down your vehicle surfaces like your steering wheel, gear shift or console. Try to use your speaker phone or a headset if possible so your phone is not continually pressed up against your cheek.

Keep Your Hair Off Your Face
This may be difficult for most of you, especially if you use your hair to help disguise your cheek jaw line blemishes. However, the oils from your hair can be an aggravating factor in acne, so it only makes sense to give your skin as much opportunity to breathe as freely and as unobstructed as possible. Try at least to keep your hair off of your face at home if you can't bring yourself to do it at work or school, or if you can't wear your hair up for professional reasons. I keep my hair up in a top bun or in cornrows away from my face whenever possible. The only time I wear my hair down is if I'm going somewhere special; once I'm home, away goes the hair.

Wash your Hair More Often

I know this sounds counterintuitive to black women. We've been raised not to wash our hair more than once every other week. However, a search of any of the reputable hair blogs on the internet will dispel this myth; washing your hair more often will not strip it of its natural oils if you use the right products; in fact, it has been shown to make your hair healthier! A clean scalp is essential to a cleaner face and therefore fewer breakouts. Also, product build up can lead to clogged pores along your forehead and jaw line. I'm not going to get into what you should and shouldn't use to care for your hair, but I will advise you that if you want to cut down on unnecessary breakouts, you need to be more conscientious about your hair in relation to your face. I try to wash (well, co-wash – look the term up) my hair twice a week and find it is much easier to keep my face breakout free as a result.

This includes weaves, because they are still attached to your head and probably come in contact with your face more than your own hair. You should keep your sewn-in hair (and your hair underneath) just as clean as if you were wearing your own hair, though I don't recommend washing it quite as often. If you wear glued in tracks, try not to exceed two weeks. Wigs should be washed around every 6-8 wears.

Change Your Pillow Case Often

Your pillowcase is in contact with your face nightly. This means whatever products you have on your face each night (including dead skin, and your natural oils), plus hair products and/or oils from your hair are all picked up by your pillow case and accumulate each night in your warm bed over the course of however many days your pillowcase is on your bed. All of these things find their way back onto your face, clogging your pores and setting the stage for future breakouts. I know it sounds excessive, but if you change your pillow case every other night (and your sheets at least every other week), you will decrease your exposure to potential acne-causing bacteria and give your face a chance to breathe at night and recuperate when the body does its repair work. I buy individual and sets of pillowcases to change mine every couple of days so I don't wear out the ones that come with the sheet set. I also wear a satin head tie (not cotton; it will dry out your hair) every night so my hair is away from my pillow and my face while asleep. You can purchase them in many colors at Target, Bobby's, Dollar Tree, or whatever discount retailer you have locally. You can also purchase them online from Amazon or eBay.

Remove Your Jewelry Every Night

Jewelry should be the last thing you put on and the first thing you take off. I'm not sure where that advice comes from, but it's good advice. Many people don't remove their earrings and necklaces every night, but we never give thought to how hygienic this practice is. Between makeup, shed skin, natural oils and perspiration, jewelry can be a breeding ground for bacteria and other microbes that remain in contact with your skin overnight, promoting breakouts on the chest and neck, behind the ears and/or the sides of the neck below the earlobes.

I was guilty of this habit, unaware of the damage I was doing to my skin until I noticed a pattern; every time I kept my jewelry on for a few days, I'd notice little breakouts in the jewelry areas – areas of my body I don't normally break out. Now, I only wear jewelry when I'm going out or for work and I take it off before my nighttime ritual. Each week, I soak all the jewelry I wore in a small bowl of hot water and liquid hand soap mixed with a couple of drops of tea tree oil (for its highly antimicrobial properties) overnight. Of course, this last bit isn't advisable for non-precious metals, this will probably only work for silver and gold jewelry. Just making it a habit to remove our jewelry at the end of the day is sufficient.

Do Not Pick ... Treat

We've all been there. A juicy, swollen whitehead or a big and obvious blackhead is on your face. It's begging to be leveled off with a squeeze between two fingers. But I'm begging you to resist the temptation to pick! Now, I'd be a hypocrite to advise you to leave it alone like the experts do – it's damn near impossible. Even when I could muster the self-control to abstain from squeezing (usually on extended stays at home when no one would see me anyway, times when it was just too painful to go through with, or just not ripe enough yet) I've found that I had the same end result. After it "healed," I still had a dark spot and maybe a couple of new eruptions developed nearby. Still, picking at the pimples will result in more damage, longer healing time and deeper, darker spots when the area does eventually recover. Not to mention the months of waiting for the spot to fade away and the eventual gaping pore left behind.

I know you don't want that. I don't want that *for* you. This is why I suggest you treat the pimple – then extract it *only* if necessary.

The first thing you need to do is identify which type of eruption it is. Is it a blackhead wedged in your pore (also known as a comedone)? Here's what to do:

1. Cleanse the area in warm water with a gentle cleanser (Cetaphil, Olay Total Effects, or Neutrogena Ultra Gentle Hydrating Cleanser for example … we'll discuss cleansers further in Chapter 8).
2. Gently blot the area dry with a clean towel used exclusively for your face or, better yet, a paper towel.
3. Fold and wrap toilet paper (or cotton rounds/squares) around the tips of your index fingers. Put each wrapped finger alongside the eruption, surrounding it, but not right on it. You kind of want to be pointing your fingers at it on both sides (but avoid using your finger nails; in fact, don't even bother trying this is you have long nails).
4. Gently press your fingers together to apply pressure under the comedone to bring it to the surface. Wiggle the fingers against the skin back and forth to gently loosen it from the skin.
5. Once it comes to the surface, if it hasn't just come out, use a tweezer to pull it out the rest of the way.
6. Clean the extraction area to avoid infection and reduce any inflammation.
7. Leave the area alone, clean and product free. Dab a little diluted Tea Tree oil or some Witch Hazel on the area if you have it on hand.

Are you dealing with a whitehead (also known as a pustule)? This will require a little more patience.

1. Keep the area clean and dry for as many days as possible. If it isn't ripe, it will hurt like hell and leave a nasty scar that will take much longer to heal. Apply a little Visine (soak a cotton swab with it) to the eruption for about 5 minutes to decrease the redness and swelling. Try to avoid makeup over the area if possible; if you can't, use a mineral or an oil-free makeup foundation. Follow up with concealer after the foundation so you're not wiping off your coverage with foundation.
2. If the eruption has not subsided days later you will either have a ripe whitehead ready to extract or one that's drying up and on its way out. In either event, follow previous

steps 2 through 4 from above to remove the debris. Keep this up until all of the debris is removed and you can't see any more coming up, but don't injure the skin or extract until you bleed. This shouldn't be painful (if it is, see Step 1 again).
3. Once it comes out, use a cotton pad soaked with antiseptic (I like hydrogen peroxide, tea tree oil diluted with water, or witch hazel) to clean the extraction area and to prevent infection.
4. Leave the area alone, clean and moisturized with an oil free moisturizer or a dab of Vitamin E oil so it doesn't scar.

Use Comedone Extractors With Caution

A comedone extractor is a small metal tool with a hole (or loop) of different sizes on each end. Its purpose is to help force more comedone material out of your pores than you could with your fingers quickly and with minimal damage to the surrounding skin. Extractors are a nifty invention, helpful in the fight against blemishes. The problem is they sometimes do more harm than good because you end up applying it to everything you see on your face and it can injure your skin more than if you'd just wrapped tissue around your fingers or used cotton swabs (or, better, left them alone). Some experts say if you have one to just throw it away but that is rash and desperate. I mean, we're not talking about a chocolate bar here…

I used to be addicted to my comedone extractor. I had congestion along my jaw line and cheeks that I obsessed over, so I always attacked it with my extractor to help smooth my skin surface. However, I was so aggressive in my extraction, I applied more pressure than necessary trying to remove each comedone completely. Plus, it was so easy to grab, I often didn't prepare my face beforehand. I ended up with a face full of dark spots that took months to fade and I had to cover with makeup, which was just as bad as the congestion I was trying to rid myself of. I tried to scale back and not be so aggressive with my extraction, but each time, I made the same mess of my face. It was a vicious cycle, but throwing out my extractor was not an option for me. For starters, I didn't like the idea of discarding a perfectly good tool I spent good money on. Mostly though, I knew the extractor wasn't the problem - I was - and I needed to work on that.

Looking back, I don't recall exactly how I weaned myself off my extractor addiction, but the first step was acknowledging I had a problem and that I needed to back off my skin if I wanted to see a difference. I still have my extractor, but I use it very seldom.

Your comedone extractor can be a valuable tool in taking care of your skin. In fact, some spas use it as part of their facials to gently and quickly rid the face of excess sebum. I think if you have one, you should keep it, but put it away someplace you can't get to it easily so you're not using it for something your fingers can't handle. But really, if your fingers can't handle it easily, you should leave it alone and not try to extract it at all. Reserve your extractor for something either really easy to remove but tiny, or something old and deep that hasn't come out on its own over time.

Keep Makeup & Equipment Up To Date

Makeup has a pretty good shelf life, but it doesn't last until the container is empty. Makeup has an expiration date, like any product that comes in a container from a manufacturer. Old makeup changes color and consistency and can possibly cause breakouts, or infection. I know makeup can be expensive, but it's not worth the possible risk to your skin health trying to hold on to makeup that has expired. To learn how to find out the expiration (or period after opening) date of our makeup, visit www.checkcosmetic.net; they provide a pretty comprehensive yet easy to understand explanation.

As for makeup brushes, cosmetic pads and other tools used to apply makeup, they should be cleansed weekly (or discarded, if it's a disposable pad or sponge) with a detergent like dishwashing liquid and left to air dry before using again. I like to put my newly cleansed brushes bristle-side up in a designated cup so the bristles aren't touching anything. Cleaning your instruments regularly helps keep bacteria out of your make up and allows your face to fight the acne without the extra burden of having to fend off other opportunistic intruders looking to destroy your complexion.

So, what do you think? Not so bad, right? Don't look at this list as more things to do in your busy life. Try to see them as new lifestyle to adapt to in your journey to defeating acne breakouts and towards clearer skin and better health! I'm willing to bet if you try any or most of these tips you will, at the very least, see a decrease in active breakouts.

BEFORE

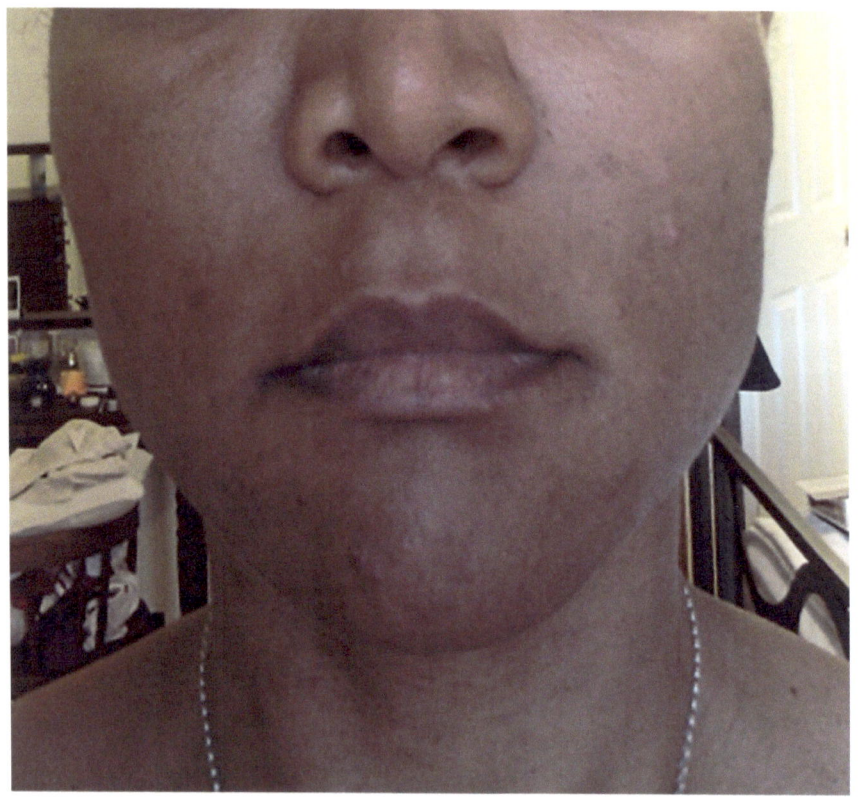

*All photos taken with my mobile phone. No retouching at all.
(Excuse the messy background!)*

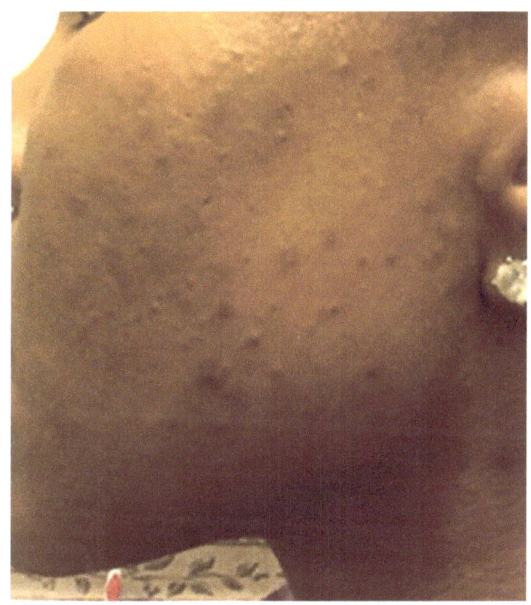
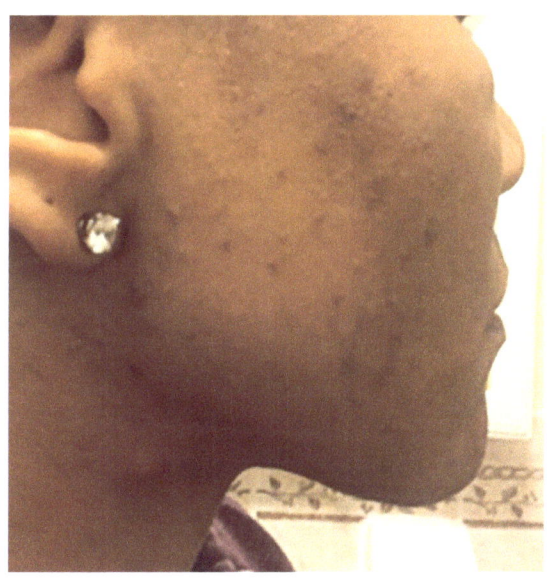

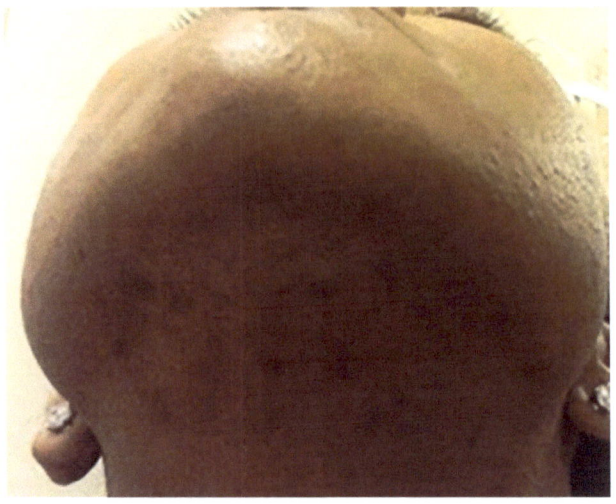

Even with medical intervention and spa treatments, my breakouts persisted. Note how the breakout extends beyond my face and the inflamed bumps on my neck.

DURING

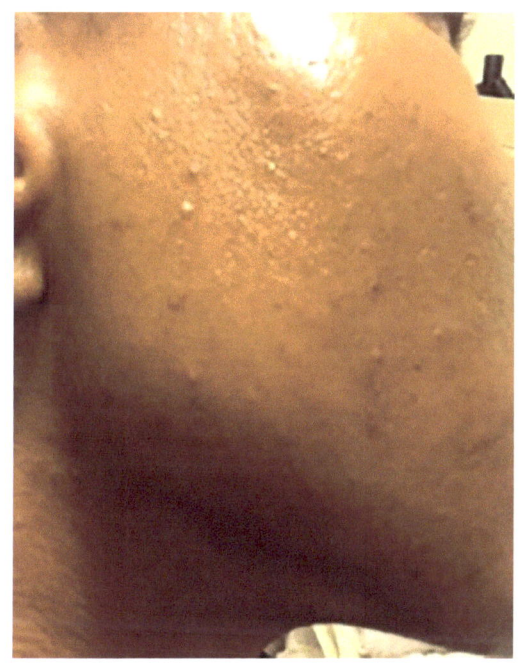

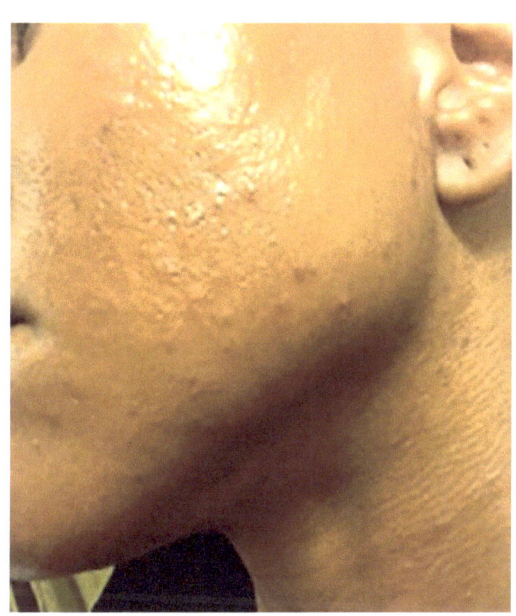

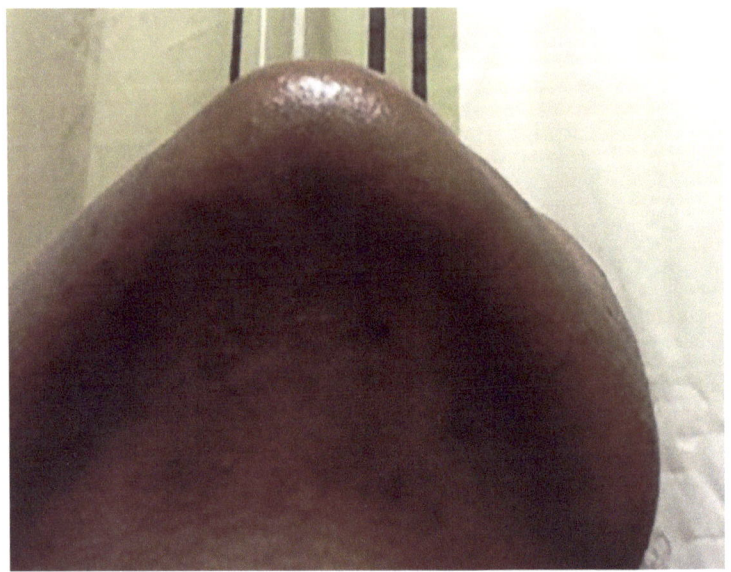

After taking matters into my own hands, you can see improvement in pigmentation and inflammation of skin. Jawline/under-the-chin acne usually takes the longest to improve however; I'm not sure why that is.

AFTER

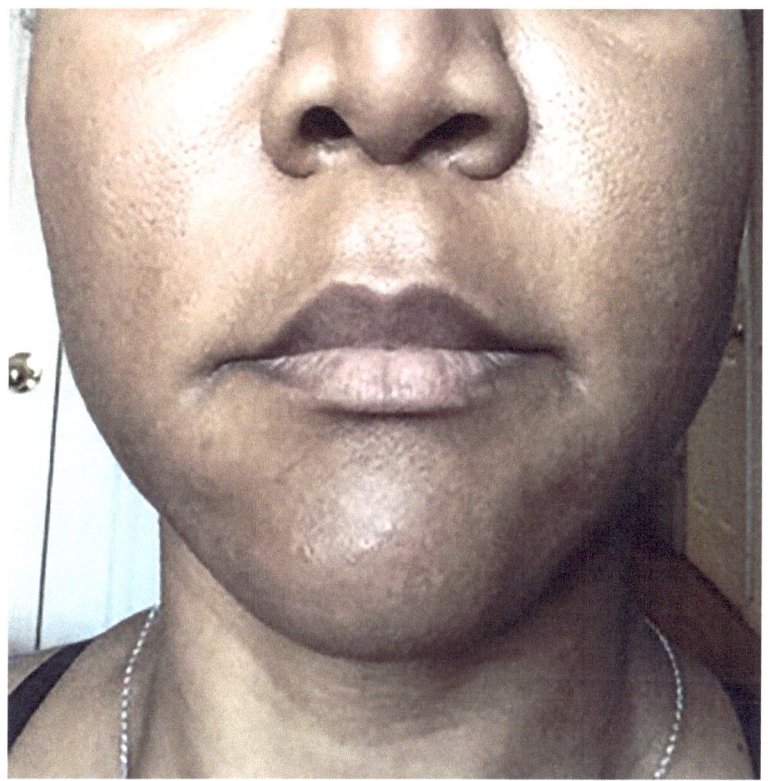

Took these photos right after having a HydraFacial, so my pores are more pronounced here than usual. But you can see that the inflammation, major congestion and hyperpigmentation are gone.

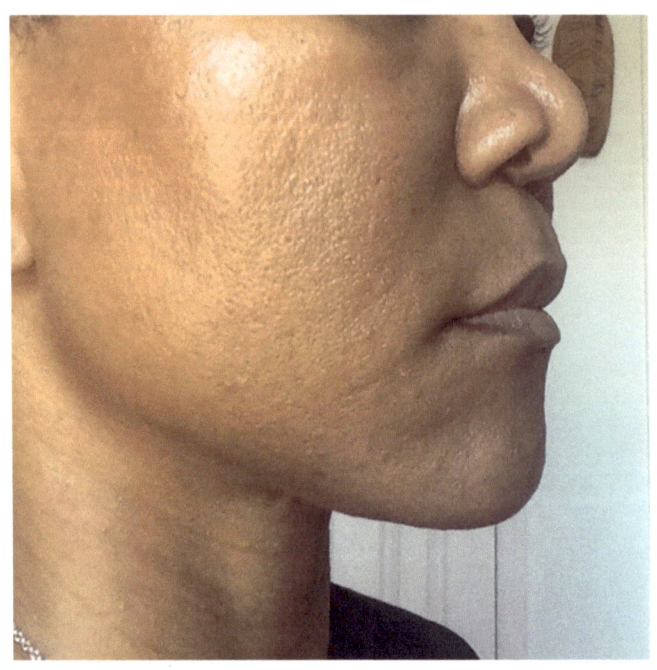
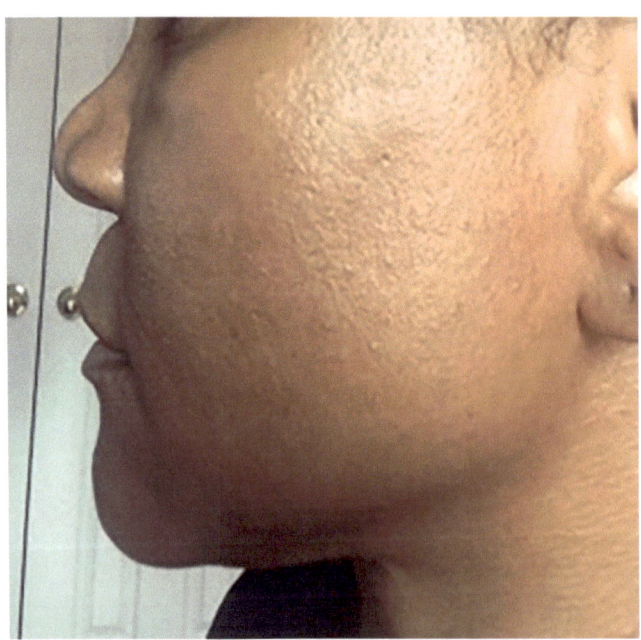

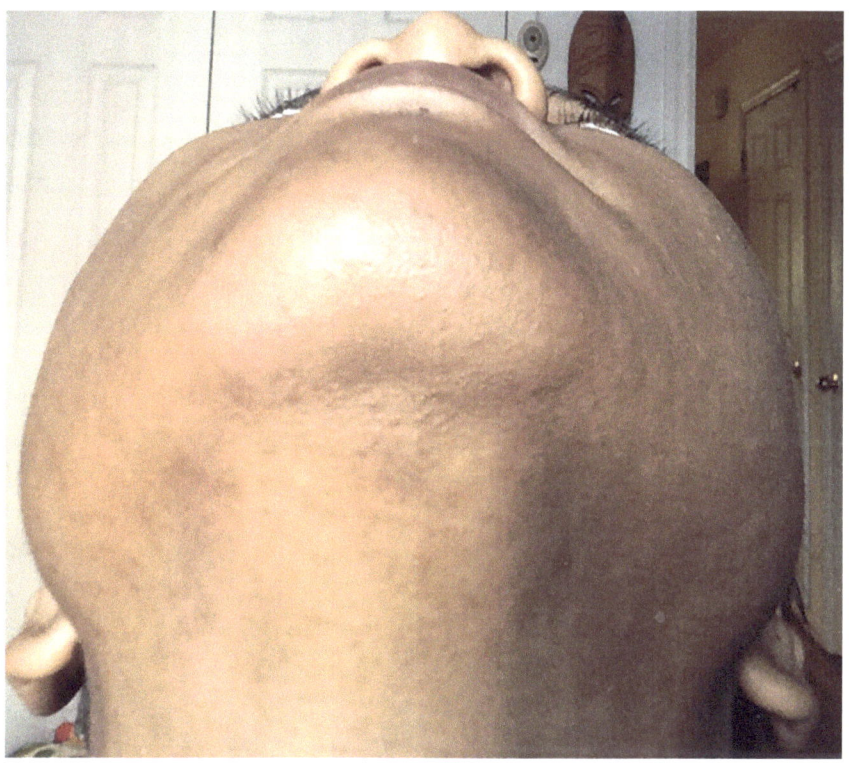

You can see that compared to the previous photos, there is vast improvement in pigmentation and oil production. I've recently learned that the skin under the chin is drier than the rest of the face, so it's possible my products don't have enough opportunity to absorb between clothing and nighttime bedding.

7
GET FIT FOR YOUR FACE

I don't think I'll have as much to say about exercise. It's such an individual choice for each person. Some people like a high intensity, heart-pounding workout. Others feel like they get plenty of exercise chasing their little ones around the house. Still others are like, "*Um, no. Just, no.*" Whatever your speed, just know this: regular exercise is essential to taming your acne. So, I'm going to assume that you have no working knowledge of (or desire to discuss) physical fitness as I write this. You can ignore this chapter if you want, but at the very least hear me out…

As I mentioned previously, exercise improves the flow of blood to your skin, delivering nutrients and carrying away waste. Sweating helps detoxify your skin, which is your biggest organ. Since toxins are a contributor to acne breakouts, it would stand to reason that the more you remove from the body, the less incidences of breakouts you'll encounter. I remember growing up my acne was much milder in high school than it was in middle school. Looking back, I realize it's because I was always active in physical education (aka gym class) and I participated in numerous team sports after school. I walked briskly to school each morning and I worked weekends as a cashier. In college, my hectic schedule left no time for exercise or any activity outside of work and studying in the library, so my complexion suffered. Today, I try to make it a priority to stay active, whether it's walking my dog or cleaning my house from top to bottom as the music plays when I can't make it to the gym. Every bit counts as long as you get off the couch and do something to get your heart rate up (that is, unless you have a medical condition that precludes you from physical activity.)

Because exercise is such a personal choice, I figured I'd make a list of exercises that you might be interested in trying to see what fits your lifestyle and level of activity. If you've never worked out in your life, you may be surprised to find something in my list that may pique your interest to try at home. If you're a gym rat and you've already found your niche, this may still be a useful resource for you, because I will include the pros and cons of each workout I list. They are in no particular order, so peruse the entire list and see what looks interesting to you.

There are 4 types of workouts:

Muscle Building

Also, known as strength training or weight training, this type of workout focuses on the major muscle groups, getting them bigger and stronger. This involves using some form of resistance equipment (weights, kettlebells, or elastic bands for example) and performing sets of repetitions (ex: 3 sets of 10; 3 sets of 15) to exert the muscles, with rest in between sets for recovery.

The best thing about muscle building exercises is that even while you rest your muscles are still burning calories (this is why some people report being hungrier after weight training) so the effects last way past the workout, increasing your metabolism. This workout also helps you lose inches in some places and gain inches in other places, depending on your goals. Another benefit is the increase in bone density because of the muscles pulling on the bones as you work out. This is a great benefit for women especially, because we tend to have smaller, less dense bones that become even smaller as we age, making us susceptible to breaks and fractures.

The downside to muscle building workouts is that you don't get the necessary cardiovascular benefits to bring more oxygen into your body. Although the muscles become stronger and more defined, if you have fat laying over them, this definition won't be visible. Aerobic exercise's cardiovascular benefits help with burning this fat.

Another drawback is that oftentimes, flexibility is lost as the muscle fibers shorten from the repetitious contraction of the muscles. Stretching before any workout is always important and can help with this issue.

Depending on your aesthetics, the bulkier looking physique acquired from classic weight training may be unappealing to some people, particularly to women who may consider the look "masculine". Experts suggest doing more reps at a lower weight to avoid this (ex: four reps of 10 at 50 lbs. instead of 3 sets of 10 at 80 lbs.).

Here are popular Muscle Building workouts:
-Weightlifting (dumbbells, machines)
-Resistance bands
-Kettlebell[7]

Cardiovascular

Also known as cardio, aerobics, or endurance training is activity that increases your breathing and heart rate to improve your endurance. Activities can range from jogging or brisk walking to running up and down flights of stairs to jumping rope. Cardiovascular has so many benefits but the main ones are improved heart health which cuts your risk of heart disease; overall weight loss due to its fat burning capabilities; decreases overall stress; and – stop me if you've heard this already - the increased blood flow to the skin nourishes and detoxifies skin (Just be sure to shower and cleanse after your workout! Sweat has been known to cause breakouts if left on the skin[8]).

Some challenges with cardio can include injury to joints, sprains, strains and muscle pulls. Another challenge with cardio is

---

[7] Kettlebells straddle disciplines. It's used in ballistic exercise which provides strength training, cardiovascular and flexibility benefits. I put it with weight training because although it's multi-discipline, kettlebells come in different weights, much like the other weight equipment.

[8] To find out more - http://www.doctorgoodskin.com/ds/acne/mechanica.php

muscle loss, which happens as your body uses protein as a last resort fuel source. Depending on your aesthetics, this could be a very good thing (if you're thrilled to lose some excess bulk), or a very bad thing (if you're not keen on the thought of your booty disappearing). Fitness experts suggest having a protein shake before any high intensity cardio activity. Or, you could simply pace yourself (ex: jog 1.5 miles instead of 3 miles).

Popular Cardiovascular workouts include:
-Jogging
-Stair Climbing
-Aerobics
-Bicycle riding

Flexibility

Flexibility exercises stretch your muscles help you stay limber and provide you with a wider range of motion. This is important for movement, balance and for preventing injuries. The most popular flexibility workout is Yoga, but Yoga's other benefit is its stress-relieving and organ cleansing properties, which are shown to have a positive effect on skin. Pilates is another example of a workout that incorporates flexibility and balance; it also tones muscles creating a longer, leaner physique. Both Yoga and Pilates help improve posture, which is good for better breathing and getting more oxygen into the body. Plus, you just look better when you stand up straighter!

The downside to flexibility workouts like Yoga and Pilates are the expense in learning how to do the poses or movements properly. There are free resources online to learn and routines you can follow at home, but that presupposes you have the means (or the discipline) to do so. If you can afford it, consider beginner DVDs or inexpensive group classes so a professional can show you the correct form from the start.

So, which type of workout do you currently do? Which type seems most interesting to you? I haven't covered every workout; for example, I didn't include martial arts, because it is primarily a form of self-defense although it has physical and mental health benefits. I didn't include High Intensity Interval Training, Barre or other workouts that require specific training, skills and equipment. I wanted to give you a cursory overview of your options. I can tell you from personal experience that I've done each type of workout at some point in my life as my aesthetics and budget changed. After many years (and thousands of dollars) I will admit that while I don't enjoy sweating, I have received the best results from a *combination* of all three workout types. Without raising my core temperature and heart rate, I was unable to really get that good detoxifying sweat I needed to help with clearing up my skin (although sitting in a steam room/sauna accomplishes that for you if you have access to one). I do Yoga or Pilates one day, I run on the treadmill another day and I do Kettlebells the next workout day.

Whatever you do, I'd like to urge you to do something at least 75 minutes a week, even if it's just jumping rope. The benefits to your skin will be a direct reflection of your physical health improving. You'll feel good inside and look good outside!

8
SKINCARE MISCONCEPTIONS

Before I start, I want to clear up a few misconceptions about acne-prone skin:

Oil Should Be Avoided – Except for mineral oil or petrolatum, this couldn't be further from the truth. Some of you may be old enough to remember Naomi Campbell famously saying years ago that uses Vaseline (petrolatum, aka petroleum jelly) on her skin to moisturize. Please understand though – Naomi Campbell *does not* have acne-prone skin. In fact, I don't know of any successful models that have acne-prone skin. I understand the temptation to want to emulate the habits of people with beautiful clear skin, but the beautiful clear skin they have is due to genetics. Mineral oil will clog your pores and exacerbate your acne. (Ok, I'll get off my soapbox now.)

Essential oils are highly beneficial to acne-prone skin. Don't forget, acne skin creates excess oil to compensate for the oil it thinks it's not getting. Applying natural oils to your skin eventually send the message to your skin that it doesn't need to send more oil to the surface. Also, many essential oils have extras that assist with wound healing like Vitamin E; you just have to use the *right* essential oils for acne-prone skin so they don't clog your pores (I discuss this in the next Chapter).

Wash Face Daily With Soap – Soap should be avoided if you can help it. The detergents in many of these soaps strip the skin of necessary oils (which, of course, signals to your skin to create more oil) and exacerbates acne. I know it sounds counter-intuitive, but a squeaky-clean face is *absolutely not* conducive to combating acne (no matter what those commercials with shiny, flawless teenagers smiling as they splash their faces with water say). Creamy cleansers (they don't have to make suds, you don't need them) and/or just plain water are perfectly acceptable to cleanse the face without drying out the skin. I mentioned MSM soap in Chapter 5 as being a great soap for acne at an economical price. My strong advice is that you avoid using soap on the face altogether, but many acne sufferers have reported success using MSM soap or African black soap to clear up their breakouts (I use the former for my bathing soap). As part of the right skin care regimen, I suppose you have nothing to lose giving either of them a try since they are specialty soaps that don't break the bank. Otherwise, please stick to cleansers.

All Lotions Are The Same – Again, simply not true. You don't have to spend a c-note on those expensive face lotions at the mall, the spa or at cosmetic chains, but I don't recommend you use regular store body or hand lotion on your face either. In fact, some lotions will state on their label what their lotion is to be used for. Body and hand lotions have different jobs than facial lotion. Body lotions have one goal and one goal only – moisturize skin on the body. Hand lotion is usually made of a heavier formula than body lotion because hands get washed more often than any other part of the body (ideally) and requires more *and* frequent hydration. Face lotion (or face cream) comes in a myriad of different formulations specific to skin types and concerns. Skin on the face is thinner than body skin and, unlike your body, it's exposed to the elements year-round.[9] Ingredients that are acceptable in a body lotion, may either create issues for the skin of your face or do nothing at all to help it. Please don't let anyone tell you that you're wasting money using different types of lotions.

Only Your Dermatologist Should Treat Your Acne – This one is difficult to dispute because it depends on how bad your acne is,

---

[9] Side note: If you suffer from back acne, you'll probably need to use a lotion that is specifically created to treat back/body acne depending on how severe it is. Facial acne treatment tends to be a milder formulation and would not be potent enough for back/body treatment.

what type of acne you have and your comfort level with caring for your own skin. If you have Demodex for example, you could use a sulfur soap to treat the infestation, but you won't know that's what you have unless you are diagnosed by a dermatologist, in which event he or she will prescribe something for you to use to treat the condition. There are many wonderful and helpful dermatologists in the world who want you to have your best skin. There are many dermatologists who see acne as not that serious when compared to melanomas or psoriasis. Then there are dermatologists who - let's be honest - have a business to run and see your skin concerns as an opportunity for recurring revenue and cosmetic procedure up sells. It doesn't mean they can't help you, it just means it could cost you more than you have or are willing to spend. I've had the pleasure of being seen by some of the best dermatologists in New York City, but I either spent a small fortune seeing them and eventually couldn't keep up, or they couldn't get me past a certain point in my treatment goal (in my mind, if I still need to wear concealer to run errands after 4 months of treatment, I've wasted my time). Also, the more cutting-edge procedures and prescription medications are not covered by insurance *and* prohibitively expensive. Many popular treatments on the market are not suitable for ethnic skin, like certain laser treatments, despite the advances in this area. If you have a disposable income and can see through the treatments a doctor will prescribe, I say it certainly can't hurt. In fact, if you've never been formally diagnosed with acne, seeing a dermatologist should be your first step to determine what type of acne you have (if it's even acne at all). I just believe that everyone is entitled to better skin than they currently have, at every budget. So, I guess what I'm really saying is you know yourself enough to know what you need, so you should decide for yourself whether you believe a dermatologist is your only option to treat your acne.

There are more misconceptions, but they might be a little too exotic to get into here. For example, I'm a big believer in regular internal cleanses (e.g., colonics, castor oil, salt water flush[10]) as

---

[10] A salt water flush is a mixture of sea salt and distilled water said to cleanse the entire digestive tract. It is purportedly a cheaper, more effective alternative

part of a skin care regimen, but that's my personal choice and I wouldn't necessarily recommend it for everybody. Many Eastern cultures consider regular internal cleansing an integral part of total health. As a little girl, my mother would give my brother and me each a spoonful of castor oil once a month, so I grew up with cleansing. However, western cultures frown on this practice, citing that your body is equipped to eliminate on its own and the risk of your colon's natural bacterial flora being thrown out of balance among other things. The point is, while I'm an advocate for the practice, it's a big commitment and, it's not completely necessary, especially if you change your diet for the better, drink plenty of water and stick with the changes.

---

to colonics, but if it's not done properly, you could end up putting stress on your kidneys. Do an internet search for "Salt Water Flush" to learn more about this regimen.

9
TOOLS FOR YOUR SKINCARE ROUTINE

The keys to clearing up your acne include, but are not limited to, the following steps:

Cleanse
Exfoliate
Moisturize

Cleansing is basically keeping the face (including the neck and ears) free of debris, such as makeup or other excess product. It does not mean making your face skin sudsy and washing until it is free of oil. Cleansing of the face skin does not even have to be done daily (I know, that sounds gross, but hear me out) because your face does not always require cleansing. Using water only to rinse your otherwise debris-free face is perfectly acceptable as is not doing anything to the face when you wake up in the morning after cleansing the night before. Of course, if you're heading out, you should wear a good oil-free sunscreen, but we'll talk about that when I get to the subject of moisturizing. For those of you that find the idea of not washing your face daily unacceptable, you should use a mild, suds-free cleanser that is creamy and gentle on the skin. I know many people of color have talked of the success they've had clearing up their skin with black soap, which does make suds. If that works for you, congratulations; just make sure you follow up with a really good moisturizer afterwards. My experience with black soap was it initially cleared up my skin, but after a few days of use my skin became uncomfortably dry and irritated, then I still had oily skin throughout the day and subsequent breakouts for my troubles. It was a vicious cycle with no end in sight of dry tight skin that burned followed by more pimples. I don't recommend using soap if you also want to curtail the extra oil production of the face, which is one of the main underlying causes of acne breakouts. Soft, supple skin should be your goal because soft supple skin retains moisture better, heals faster and breaks out much less. I recommend cleansers that have a consistency like Phisoderm or Cetaphil, or that have a gel or cream consistency but makes very little if any suds. They don't feel like they're doing much, especially when you're removing makeup, but these types of cleansers have been prescribed by dermatologists for years because they are consistently shown to be gentle on facial skin. Micellar water is also a good product to use before your gentle cleanser to remove makeup. When skin is injured or damaged, the last thing you want to do is dry it out. Think about when you get a cut; it heals better when you put some antibiotic ointment on it because clean, moist skin heals itself better. We've all been conditioned for years that a sudsy wash that makes your face oil free is the standard, but this would be a good time to unlearn that habit if you want to see your acne clear up for once and for all.

Another type of cleanse you can do for your skin is an oil cleanse. This involves the use of an essential oil (or an oil mixture) of your choice massaged into your skin for several minutes. Then, you apply a clean hot face towel to your oily massaged face for several minutes, letting the steam and the oil penetrate before gently removing the oil from your face with the cloth. I know it may sound weird, but oil cleansing with essential oils is an excellent way to balance your skin and provide it with essential moisture that helps curtail over production of oil and sebum. Just make sure you're using essential oils like Jojoba, Grapeseed or Argan oil for example. Natural castor oil (not the stuff you find in the pharmacy) is also an excellent moisturizer for troubled skin. Coconut oil is iffy because some people swear by it, while others report it tends to be comedogenic (clogs pores). The important thing to know is the balance of Linoleic acid to oleic acid in your oil; acne prone and congested skin tend be deficient in Linoleic acid, creating the clogged pores we're all too familiar with that is composed primarily of oleic acid. Linoleic acid oils are known for breaking up that dried sebum, leading to less congestion and less breakouts. One of my favorite blogs Minimalist Beauty, talks about this and provides a very helpful list of essential oils and their percentages of linoleic to oleic acids. Remember though, this is about learning what your skin responds to or rejects so you can create a regimen that is right for *you*. Whatever you do, please avoid oils like mineral oil or petrolatum

Exfoliating is the removal of layers of epidermis or top skin layer to bring the newer, fresher skin underneath to the surface and to increase cell turnover. This is essential to acne prone skin because it helps remove the layers of dead skin that we are not able to naturally shed like people with normal skin. There are two types of exfoliation: mechanical and chemical.

Mechanical exfoliation is achieved using scrubs, brushes or sponges. Examples of each would be a facial wash with tiny little particles in the wash that feel grainy to the touch; a bristle brush made specifically for use on the face with a cleanser (same principal as brushing your teeth); and a textured type sponge like a loofah or other naturally rough surface. *Chemical exfoliation* uses a chemical (usually an acid formula) to remove layers of skin over time.

Both methods have their pros and cons. Mechanical exfoliation is less expensive and can theoretically be used more often on the skin, but there is high possibility of injuring your skin by exposing it to abrasive products or by over doing it. I have found baking soda (yes, just good old-fashioned Arm & Hammer) to be a terrific exfoliating scrub that doesn't leave your skin tender afterwards. Bioré makes a baking soda scrub that I love to use, but save your money and stick to the original. Chemical exfoliation gives a much better result and doesn't have to be used as often, but many require professional services and can be expensive. For our intents and purposes, I will only talk about products that are easy and safe to use at home on your own.

I will come clean here and admit that I do administer my own chemical exfoliation at home; I have had extensive exposure to chemical exfoliation from my many years of dermatologist and aesthetician treatments so I feel comfortable doing them myself.

However, I *strongly* recommend against this practice because of the potential for serious injury from chemical burns you can inflict on yourself. Just because it's available on the open market doesn't make it safe to use at home. Acids like high percentage Glycolic Acid or TCA (Trichloroacetic Acid) are serious business and should only be administered by a trained professional. (I feel as if I'm talking out of two sides of my face here... I guess I'm just trying to be honest with you. But I am *not* a professional aesthetician. I dislike when people claim their beauty or fitness routine required nothing more than basic steps when they clearly look like they've spent hours and countless dollars to achieve their results. Take my word for it, please. See your licensed aesthetician or your cosmetic dermatologist to get this procedure done right. Most "at-home" treatments leave a lot of instruction out that are essential to the proper application and removal of acid formulas and there are some parts to the procedure that require knowing what to look for, which is different for every individual.)

That said, there are some pretty awesome acids that are formulated for home use. Hydroxy acids (lactic acid, low percentage glycolic acid or salicylic acid for example) are great for effective exfoliating and can be found in many cleansers and moisturizers made especially for acne-prone skin. The trick is to use them regularly to keep dead skin at bay and keep your pores clear so you don't over produce sebum. I use a cream cleanser that contains glycolic acid (a glycolic wash) to cleanse my face and I alternate between using my Clarisonic (it's a scrubbing brush that vibrates on the skin, made from the same technology that created the Sonicare toothbrush and operates using the same principal of gentle cleansing) and using my glycolic toner (that contains 5% glycolic acid) to help sweep away dead skin after I cleanse if my skin still feels like it needs some help[11]. Many people are in love

---

[11] Proactiv also makes a deep cleansing brush that costs much less than Clarisonic; they offer it with their skin care system. I'm personally not a fan of Proactiv's automatic monthly billing. If I'm going to get billed monthly, I prefer Rx For Brown Skin; I find it gentler and better on dark spots than Proactiv's system. However, I don't believe Rx has a skincare brush.

with salicylic acid products because of how gentle they are and how easy it is to find them in common skincare products. Clearasil and Neutrogena, for example, use salicylic acid in their products at very reasonable prices. However, in my experience, I have found their formulations focus too much on oil removal and as I've mentioned, that should not be your goal if you want to balance your skin and tame your acne. Of course, it could work if you follow up with a great hydrating moisturizer afterwards, but I really recommend that you find a cream cleanser with salicylic acid that doesn't contain detergents like sodium lauryl sulfate or sodium laureth sulfate that can strip your skin of its natural oils. After you rinse the cleanser from your face, dab or pat your face dry with a clean towel you use only for your face or with a paper towel; never wipe your face dry, you'll only end up over-drying your skin and laying the ground work to create premature wrinkles.

A product that I really like for home exfoliating is *Cure Natural Aqua Gel*. It's a Japanese exfoliating clear liquid/gel product that you can use at home by yourself. I found this product when I was pregnant and nervous about using any of my acids to maintain my skin. It doesn't burn on application; you can just use your hands and rub it into your cleansed, patted dry facial skin to mechanically remove dead skin. The great thing about Cure is you almost can't make a mistake. You can't leave it on too long and it's self-limiting; you can see the dead skin beading off as you massage it onto your face and when you can't remove any more you simply rinse it all off with lukewarm water. Just make sure to avoid you eye area and your mouth completely; the skin around the eyes and on your lips, are too thin and delicate and you don't want to expose them to products that aren't exclusively made for those areas. You can find out more about it through online beauty retailers.[12]

Moisturizing is the act of applying an emollient of some sort to

---

[12] I am not paid to endorse this product, nor am I affiliated with the company or its retailers in any way. I just think it's a good product based on my experience (even if the instructions on the label are in Japanese).

the cleansed face, neck and décolleté (cleavage). It can be an (essential) oil or an oil free cream moisturizer (by oil free, manufacturers generally mean no mineral oil or petrolatum that can clog your pores), but the goal is to keep the skin hydrated on the outside after cleansing so it can work effectively to protect from breakouts and to heal itself from previous and future damage. Exfoliation helps speed up the cell turnover and speed healing of scars and dark spots, but moisturizing is the key to breaking the cycle of oil over production, which cuts back on break outs, which reduces the amount of acne and subsequent acne scarring and dark spots to begin with.

Whether you use an oil or a cream to moisturize, it's best to apply moisturizer to your face while it's still a little damp from cleansing. Rub it into your hands first to warm it up so that it goes on easily and absorbs into your skin. I like to gently spread my moisturizer outwards over my face (nose to ears) and let my warm hands sit on my face for a while with the lotion. Don't be afraid to gently massage your face while you moisturize; it's a great way to bring blood flow to your face and it helps drive the moisturizer deeper into your skin. When you apply your makeup to your moisturized skin it will look more natural and blend better (provided you have the right color for your skin, that is…) because you will have a better base to work with.

Once you get your moisture game down pat and you skin looks and feels more balanced (i.e., not shiny from over-production of oil, feels supple and non-greasy to the touch) you won't even need to wash your face daily. I always make sure to cleanse at night, especially if I've been out that day or wore makeup. Most mornings however, I don't bother to cleanse my face; I just apply my sunscreen and get on with my other activities. Of course, if you're applying makeup everyday (a practice I don't recommend, but I understand everyone's lifestyles are different) you will need to gently cleanse and moisturize daily to clear the pores of products, to prevent buildup and to have a fresh palate on which to apply your makeup each day. I'm only suggesting that if you don't wear makeup regularly, you could get to that point in your skin care regimen.

I need to take a moment to stress the use of sunscreen; it is a non-negotiable part of your moisture regimen. Many women of color believe they don't need sun protection because of melanin, the pigment that provides skin, hair and eyes with their color (in general the more melanin you have, the less likely you are to be burned by sun rays). However, just because you have darker skin doesn't mean you're immune to the effects of the sun on your skin. If you are prone to dark marks, it is even more critical that you wear sun protection because those dark marks are dark due to melanin deposited to the area once an injury occurs to the skin (a healing pimple for example). Exposure to sun triggers the production of extra melanin in skin, which is known commonly as a sun tan, but the same also happens to blemishes on your skin, so your dark marks get darker and take longer to fade. You can fight this by simply layering a good sun screen on top of your moisturizer, preferably before you apply any foundation and makeup. Most sunscreens require you to re-apply throughout the day; this is normal. Try to avoid formulations that contain zinc oxide or titanium dioxide. Most people can tolerate them just fine, but in my experience, I found them to exacerbate my acne congestion. Formulas that use oxybenzone and avobenzone seem to do a nice job of protecting skin without the comedogenic side effects. I've read that the mineral formulas (the ones containing oxides) are superior to the chemical formulas. My humble opinion is just because something is natural doesn't automatically make it better for you. But experiment with different formulas made for the face to see what works best for you if the idea of a chemical based sunscreen makes you uncomfortable. I haven't had any issues with *DDF Weightless Defense Oil-Free Hydrator UV Moisturizer*. It's fragrance free and feels so light and non-greasy on my face. I wear it daily (the SPF is 45) to protect myself from dark spots[13].

---

[13] I recently found out I'm at genetic risk for skin cancer, which makes sunscreen *even more* important to my daily regimen. Don't think for a second this only happens to white folks! Brown skin *needs* sun protection.

A great resource for how to moisturize your skin is a book called **The Japanese Skincare Revolution** by Chizu Seaki. In it, she discusses techniques for cleansing, moisturizing and massaging your face so it feels pampered and supple over time. This book is also a great resource for skincare products that won't break the bank[14] (keep in mind - you will have to spend a little extra on quality products to get started, but they pay for themselves over time and end up being much cheaper than the trial, error and disappointment of investing in trendy products that don't help you achieve results. I've spent a king's ransom on all sorts of products from the dime store to the high end and trust me when I tell you there are good affordable products on the market that work, but you will need to make a small investment and find the ones that work for you).

****

So, that's it my lovelies. You now have all the basic tools you need to tame your acne-prone complexion. I hope you will have patience with your skin, because chances are your acne didn't happen overnight. And I hope you will be disciplined in your lifestyle changes because they are the key to long-term success in your journey. Not everything I recommend in this book will work for everyone; you must create a plan that's right for you, providing you keep to the basic tenets. Less sugar, more water and better hygiene *must* be part of your plan. Moisturizing is also non-negotiable. How you put it all together is what will come to you as you go through this journey. And make no mistake – this will be a journey, filled with trial and error, with setbacks and leaps forward. In the beginning, you'll feel apprehension and maybe some regret as your skin goes from worse (this happens often when

---

[14] Again, I'm not a paid endorser, just an avid fan of the book (well, parts of it anyway). I promise you, I make nothing off these recommendations.

the skin begins to purge its contents that were hidden below the surface as it begins to heal itself) to better, but have patience and keep at it. You will tame your acne once and for all.

I really want to hear from you[15]. I welcome your comments, questions, your success stories and your setbacks.

---

[15] Unfortunately, internet trolling is real. I'm sure not everyone will agree with my advice, but I won't reply to anyone who is rude and insulting. If we can't have civil discourse, there's nothing to discuss. Just saying...

10
AFTERWORD

I wrote this book in 2014 during a creative fit after marveling at how my skin had finally improved using the simple methods in this book while all the money I spent on treatments had done nothing. Years later, my skin is still breakout-free and I'm still amazed.

I put it down for a moment, because I wanted to consider what else I could add to the book that could help cut down on acne breakouts without breaking the bank (I thought about adding micro-needling, for example, but decided against it; your skin needs to clear up first or you'll only succeed in spreading acne bacteria all over your face). During that time, however, I went through a divorce (again), had a baby, had surgery and renovated my home – pretty much back-to-back. I thought *for sure* my face was going to break out from the stress of it all, but to my continued amazement, my face survived. (A few lines have developed though!)

I thought for a while about simply not publishing this book anymore. I thought it might be pointless three years later. But then, I'd look in the mirror and remember how grateful I was that the people whose information I used to help clear up my skin even put it out there for me to find. And then I realized that there still isn't a wealth of information on acne care for those of us with melanin that didn't involve products, pills or procedures. I mean, there are great communities for healthy hair care and natural hair care, YouTube channels and message boards for days on cosmetics, products and procedures, but nothing comparable for basic acne care for brown skin.

So, I figured, *what the heck*. I went ahead and published it.

I'm not a doctor or an aesthetician, just a lifelong sufferer of acne who had tried almost everything deemed safe for my brown skin that I could afford. I haven't tried any of the laser treatments that are available for darker skin. But I have tried Microdermabrasion, Glycolic acid peels, TCA peels, HydraFacials, spa facials with extractions, clay masks, antibiotics, Retin-A, Accutane, Clearasil, Proactiv, Rx for Brown Skin and a dozen other doctor-prescribed or spa-recommended products whose names escape me as I write this. If I'm being honest, the acid peels yielded good results for me, but these treatments cost money and there never seemed to be an end in sight. I was maxing my credit cards for services that wore off a few months after the treatment stopped. The definition of insanity is doing the same things over and over looking for different results, and let me tell you: I was driving myself crazy! Perhaps if I had the money to see through a combination of procedures to clear my skin, I might not have even conceived of this book, but that wasn't the case for me. So, I had to get serious about my circumstances and find lasting solutions that I could do for myself at home.

I figured there must be people out there like myself who just decided to stop chasing the fantasy of flawless skin. And I'm telling you from experience, you do have options. You *can* stop the breakouts at home on your own time. I don't have flawless skin; years of unsuccessful treatments, extractions and stress-picking have left me with enlarged pores. But I no longer have acne lesions, a spotty complexion or overly oily skin. (Some of it could also just be me getting older, but I'll never know at this point.)

So, here I am, offering my two cents to this very big conversation, one brown person to another. And I truly hope this book will help you as much as learning all of this has helped me. I also hope that you will applaud your efforts and not set up unrealistic expectations for your results. That will set the stage for failure and I want you to succeed.

I would really love to hear from you. Please send your success stories, your setbacks, your (constructive) complaints and any general questions or advice to **yourclearestskin@gmail.com**. If I can answer your questions I will answer based on my experience on the subject and if I don't know the answer, I'll be honest and tell you so. I'm also dying to hear about other DIY fixes I may not be aware of for ethnic skin. This is still a learning process for me too!

It's better late than never, so let's start a conversation about ethnic skin! It's time for us to stop suffering on the sidelines in embarrassment. Live and love your best skin - you deserve it!

-Tamara

ABOUT THE AUTHOR

Tamara Thomas is a writer and Graphic Designer who lives in Brooklyn, New York. She graduated from New York University and enjoys reading, research and writing about subjects she finds interesting.